**At the
Top of
Their
Game**

Ichiro
Suzuki

A League of
His Own

Budd Bailey

Cavendish
Square

New York

Published in 2018 by Cavendish Square Publishing, LLC
243 5th Avenue, Suite 136, New York, NY 10016

CPSIA Compliance Information: Batch #CS17CSQ

All websites were available and accurate when this book was sent to press.

Library of Congress Cataloging-in-Publication Data

Names: Bailey, Budd, 1955- author.
Title: Ichiro Suzuki : a league of his own / Budd Bailey.
Description: New York : Cavendish Square, [2018] | Series: At the top of their game | Includes bibliographical references and index.
Identifiers: LCCN 2016059796 (print) | LCCN 2017000071 (ebook) | ISBN 9781502627605 (library bound) | ISBN 9781502627612 (E-book)
Subjects: LCSH: Suzuki, Ichiro, 1973---Juvenile literature. | Baseball players--United States--Biography--Juvenile literature. | Baseball players--Japan--Biography--Juvenile literature.
Classification: LCC GV865.S895 B35 2018 (print) | LCC GV865.S895 (ebook) | DDC 796.357092 [B] --dc23
LC record available at https://lccn.loc.gov/2016059796

Editorial Director: David McNamara
Editor: Fletcher Doyle
Copy Editor: Rebecca Rohan
Associate Art Director: Amy Greenan
Designer: Jessica Nevins
Production Coordinator: Karol Szymczuk
Photo Research: J8 Media

At the Top of Their Game

Contents

Perfect Translation

The name "Ichiro" translates from Japanese to English as "first son." This may seem a little odd in the case of baseball great Ichiro Suzuki, since he was actually the second son born to the Suzuki family of Kasugai, Japan.

But consider Ichiro's baseball career, and "first son" starts to make more sense. He wasn't the first player to go from Japan to North America, and he wasn't the first to have some great moments after crossing the ocean. But Ichiro was the best Japanese player to join Major League Baseball, breaking stereotypes along the way. Many baseball experts wondered if Japanese players were physically big enough to compete in North America. Ichiro, at five feet eleven inches (1.8 meters) and 170 pounds (77 kilograms), was no giant except when he walked onto the field.

The outfielder broke records with his bat and astonished teammates, opponents, and fans with his throwing arm and foot speed. By the end of the 2016 season, he was considered to be one of the one hundred greatest players in Major League Baseball

Opposite: Ichiro's unusual batting stance has become familiar to millions of baseball fans in many countries over the years.

history. His spot in the Baseball Hall of Fame in Cooperstown seems assured when he finally gets around to retiring.

Ichiro has had a very unusual baseball career. He spent several seasons playing in Japan's top league and dominated it. He arrived in Seattle in 2001 at the age of twenty-seven to play for the Mariners. There were some who thought the outfielder might struggle against the higher level of competition, but Ichiro quickly destroyed those thoughts. He was one of the best in the game from Day One.

Others had come from Japan to play in North America, with various degrees of success. It's not easy to make that jump. Not

Ichiro was still adding hits to his incredible career total with the Miami Marlins well past the age of forty.

Ichiro Suzuki: A League of His Own

only is the sport played differently here, but the language barrier is immense, and the cultural differences are large. Some Japanese players spent a few years here, then turned around and went back home to finish out their careers. However, there isn't much Ichiro can't do on a baseball diamond. The only fair comparison with what he did might be to players who joined Major League Baseball from the **Negro Leagues** in the 1940s and 1950s, who also started their MLB careers late but became stars.

So let's take a look at Ichiro's story in detail—how he was a star at a young age, was idolized in Japan, made a highly publicized move to Seattle, instantly played at a Hall of Fame level, and was still a useful player at the age of forty-two, going past a couple of major milestones during the 2016 season.

Putting Ichiro's career into perspective, baseball has been played in relatively few countries over the years, and almost all of them were in the Western Hemisphere. For several years, Japan was the game's lone outpost across the Pacific Ocean. The relationship between Japanese and American baseball makes Ichiro's rise even more interesting, and his story begins with one of the game's most legendary figures.

1 Beginnings

It was the fall of 1934, and Babe Ruth—baseball's greatest star at the time—had just checked into the Imperial Hotel in Tokyo. He was visiting as part of a special postseason exhibition tour of Japan by more than a dozen players, including four other future Hall of Famers such as Lou Gehrig and Jimmie Foxx.

Ruth was with his wife, Claire, and his daughter, Julia, when there was a knock at the door. Ruth answered it and was greeted by a Japanese man in a **kimono**.

"Sign baseball?" the man asked.

Ruth signed the ball, but the man pulled out another baseball to be signed. And then another, and another. After a while, it became something out of a comedy routine.

"That man must have had two dozen baseballs in the sleeves of his kimono," Julia Ruth Stevens told the *New York Times* many years later. "Daddy signed them all."

If Ruth and his fellow players had any doubts about the reception they'd receive in Japan, they had gotten their answer by the seventh or eighth baseball.

Opposite: Babe Ruth's visit to Japan for an exhibition series in 1934 did much to popularize baseball in the Far East.

"They loved Daddy over there," Stevens said. "When we rode in open cars from the Tokyo train station to the hotel, the Japanese people were waving little American flags and yelling, 'I love Bay-bee. I love Bay-bee.'"

Ruth's arrival in Japan was a huge moment in the rise in popularity of baseball there. Historians credit Hiroshi Hiraoka for creating the first Japanese baseball team in 1878. That's only two years after the National League began play in the United States and nine years after the first professional team—the Cincinnati Red Stockings—started play in 1869. Hiraoka was a railway engineer who studied in the United States, and he brought baseball back to Japan with him. His curveballs were called "magic balls" by Japanese batters who had never seen such a pitch. Hiraoka started the Shinbashi Athletic Club Athletics.

He had help in planting baseball's seeds. Horace Wilson was an English professor at what later became known as Tokyo Imperial University. He helped introduce the game to a new audience. Albert Bates, a teacher at Kaitaku University, is credited with organizing the first baseball game in Japan. Team sports were said to be unknown in Japan then, which might have created some curiosity for the game by the people there.

By the 1880s, a few high schools and colleges were playing baseball, and occasionally they'd play teams of foreigners who were living in Japan. A one-sided loss was enough to drive the young Japanese players to practice for long periods of time in an effort to improve their skills. Long workouts have been associated with Japanese sports for many years, and that work ethic is still associated with Japanese baseball today.

Big League Contact

Major League Baseball soon started to make contact with representatives of the Japanese game. A collection of pros arrived in 1908 for an Asian tour. Five years later, the Chicago White Sox and the New York Giants passed through Japan as part of a world tour.

By the start of the twentieth century, several Japanese universities had started to field teams. In an effort to get better, representatives came to the United States to learn about the sport. In return, American players and teams crossed over the Pacific to stage friendly games and clinics. That could only help the level of play, and it led to leagues and rivalries. The game between Waseda and Keio Universities quickly became intense, and eventually the games had to be stopped. The teams did not play for twenty years. Today, their games are on national television, and classes at the schools are cancelled when their teams are matched.

That brings us to an important name in Japan's baseball story: Lefty O'Doul. Ichiro Suzuki would have appreciated O'Doul. He has one of the best career batting averages in major league history at .349, and he won two batting titles along the way. O'Doul led a tour of major leaguers to Japan, the Philippines, and China in 1931. He returned in 1932 and 1933 to conduct clinics, and he helped organize the 1934 trip that brought Ruth to Japan. The Americans dispatched their Japanese opponents on that tour with ease, winning all eighteen of the games. But there was one memorable highlight. Eiji Sawamura struck out Charlie Gehringer, Babe Ruth, Lou Gehrig, and Jimmie Foxx—all future Hall of Famers—in order.

Waseda University's baseball tradition dates back about a century. This team photo was taken in 1916.

Ichiro Suzuki: A League of His Own

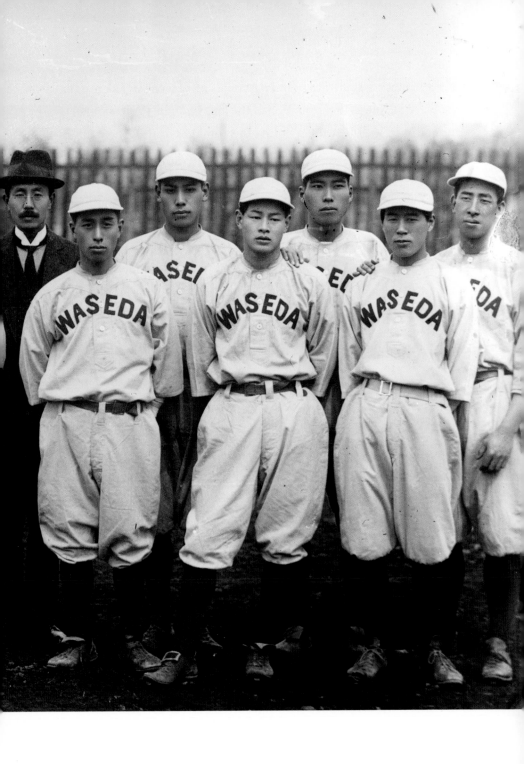

O'Doul continued to spend part of his **offseasons** in Japan, and he played a role in the formation of the first Japanese professional league in 1936. The team in Tokyo, the Yomiuri Giants, picked up its nickname as something of a tribute to O'Doul, who finished his major league career with the New York Giants in 1933–1934.

O'Doul grew to love Japan and was deeply upset when the nation turned to **militarism** in the late 1930s. He supposedly said that the Japanese attack on **Pearl Harbor** in Hawaii, which started World War II for the United States, was the saddest day of his life. Baseball was still played in Japan through the early 1940s, although the schedule eventually was reduced. The entire season was cancelled in 1945, but the game bounced back with surprising speed once World War II ended later that year. The occupying Allied forces thought the sport might do something for morale.

Barriers Cleared

Baseball in Japan still needed a boost after that, though, and O'Doul popped up again. He brought his minor league team, the San Francisco Seals of the Pacific Coast League, to Japan on a tour, and he returned several times in the 1950s. In fact, the 1951 team— managed by O'Doul—lost a game to a Japanese opponent, the first time that had ever happened to pros from the United States. O'Doul was eventually inducted into Japan's Baseball Hall of Fame. O'Doul died on December 7, 1969—twenty-eight years to the day from the Pearl Harbor attack.

Another barrier came down in 1951, when Wally Yonamine became the first American to play in the Japanese pro league. Yonamine was a Hawaiian who had played football for the

Lefty O'Doul was a great ambassador for baseball in Japan. He managed the San Francisco Seals of the Pacific Coast League after retiring in 1934.

San Francisco 49ers and was told by O'Doul that playing in Japan would work out well for him. O'Doul was right. Yonamine won four championships, played in eleven All-Star Games, and won three batting titles. He also brought an aggressive style of play to Japan that hadn't really been seen there before.

If most American baseball fans in the 1960s, '70s and '80s were asked to name one baseball player from Japan, they more than likely would have picked Sadaharu Oh. He arrived in Japan's best league in 1959, took a couple of years to get comfortable, and then went on a power spree that at least statistically has never been equaled. Oh hit 868 home runs during a spectacular twenty-two-year career. That's more than 100 ahead of Major League Baseball's leader, Barry Bonds. Even if the ballparks were smaller in Japan and the competition wasn't as good, that's still a lot of home runs. Oh led his league in homers fifteen times and was the Most Valuable Player of the Central League nine times.

Japanese Recruited

During Oh's career, Japanese players only performed in Japan—with one exception. It's an odd footnote to the story.

The city of San Francisco had a large population of Japanese-Americans in the 1960s. Giants owner Horace Stoneham figured a Japanese player would be a huge drawing card to those portions of the city. Therefore, in 1964 the team signed three young players to contracts: catcher Hiroshi Takahashi, third baseman Tatsuhiko Tanaka, and pitcher Masanori Murakami. The first two players were eighteen, while Murakami was nineteen.

Murakami quickly proved to be the best of the three in the minors, as he had a 1.78 **earned-run average**. The Giants called him up to the majors on August 31. He played against the Mets in New York the next day and was nervous like any other **rookie** when he walked in from the **bullpen** to pitch.

"I go to the fence, and the door opens, and I go in," Murakami said later to the *Guardian*. "I'm walking to the mound, that time, wow. But [being] inside [the field] is very different. Maybe if I get nervous, it's not good. Now, I think OK, make me relax. The stands, the people. I can hear [them], but I don't know what they're saying. I understood a little English."

He pitched a scoreless inning in his debut. Murakami appeared in nine games that season, going 1–0 with a 1.80 ERA and striking out fifteen against one walk. "I throw a fastball and curve, but no change," Murakami told the *Sporting News*. "The changeup is no good. Relief pitcher comes in, men are on base. If you throw a change … Boom! Long ball."

The pitcher went back and forth on his plans for 1965, at one point saying his parents back in Japan missed him and he wished to return. There were disagreements over his contract status, and it took a while to work out the situation. Murakami agreed to return to the Giants for the 1965 season, but he was free to return to Japan after that. He pitched well, appearing in forty-five games with a 4–1 record and 3.75 earned-run average, and headed home.

Murakami played seventeen more seasons in Japan. Rumors about a return to San Francisco often circulated, and they came true when he tried out for the team in 1983 at the age of thirty-eight. Murakami was one of the team's final cuts.

Birth of a Star

By 1973, no other Japanese player had tried to play in Major League Baseball, although a few Americans had gone in the other direction and played with Japanese teams to give their careers a boost. The person who would change Japanese baseball forever was born on October 22 of that year. Yoshie and Nobuyuki Suzuki of Kasugai welcomed their second son, Ichiro, into the world. The family lived in a suburb of Nagoya in the middle of the country. It's about 160 miles (257 kilometers) by air from Nagoya to Tokyo, and Mount Fuji is close to the halfway point of that trip.

Nobuyuki, Ichiro's father, had played high school baseball, and he seemed determined to see his son succeed in the sport. When Ichiro was three years old, his father gave him a glove and worked with him in the yard on his skills. By the time Ichiro was seven, he had become a member of his first team. Father and son spent hours together each day, practicing and drilling. The routine is said to have included throwing 50 pitches, fielding 50 ground balls, and 50 fly balls, and hitting 500 pitches—250 from a hitting machine and 250 from his father. Soon he had written the word "concentration" in Japanese on his glove. After dinner, they went to a **batting cage** for more work.

By the age of twelve, Ichiro had already decided to try to become a professional baseball player when he became older. He wrote this essay about his plans:

> My dream when I grow up is to be a first-class professional baseball player ... I have the confidence to do the necessary practice to reach that goal. I

started practicing from age three. From the age of nine I practiced baseball 360 out of 365 days a year and I practiced hard. I only had five to six hours a year to play with my friends. That's how much I practiced. So I think I can surely become a pro. I will play in junior high school and high school. When I graduate I will enter the pros. My dream is to join the Seibu Lions or the Chunichi Dragons. My goal is a contract-signing bonus of 100 million **yen** (about $650,000).

The sessions became even more challenging from then on. Nobuyuki has been quoted as saying that "baseball was fun for both of us." Ichiro later disagreed, saying he didn't have much fun. "It bordered on **hazing,** and I suffered a lot," he said. Sometimes in the winter, the weather was so cold that Ichiro's frozen fingers couldn't button his shirt.

The drills became almost legendary, at least among Ichiro's many fans. The speed of pitches kept getting turned up as he became more skilled at batting. The batting cage operator eventually told the boy and his father that 80 miles per hour (129 kilometers per hour) was as fast as the machine would deliver a ball. To further test the youngster's skills, the pitching device was pushed forward by several feet. That simulated the delivery of a pitch at 93 miles per hour (150 kmh). Day after day, father and son were there. They kept feeding the machine at a rate of one dollar per twenty-five pitches.

From there, it was on to high school for Ichiro. High school is the first time that athletes discover how they rank among their peers. In other words, if they can succeed at that level, they have a chance to move up the ladder as they become older.

Ichiro passed the first test when he was admitted to Aikodai Medien High School, which was known for its strong baseball program. The school had produced eleven professional players at that point. His father told his new coach, "No matter how good Ichiro is, don't ever praise him. We have to make him spiritually strong."

It's uncertain if the high school coaching staff stuck to those words, because Ichiro's performance deserved praise. His three-year varsity career was outstanding. He was mostly used as a pitcher, but his hitting attracted attention. Suzuki hit .502, with 19 home runs and 131 stolen bases. He also struck out only 10 times in 536 at-bats, and all 10 of them were on called third strikes.

Making a Name

During those high school years, Suzuki and the rest of the Aikodai Medien team had the chance to play in one of the great sporting spectacles of Japan: the Koshien—Japan's national high school baseball tournament.

There's nothing in the United States quite like this, although the NCAA Basketball Tournament probably comes

The Koshien has long been one of the highlights of Japan's annual sports calendar. This celebration happened at the tournament in the 1970s.

closest. Teams throughout Japan play off for the chance to participate in the summer tournament in Nishinomiya. The city's pro team, the Tigers, must go on a road trip for three weeks so that the tournament can be staged in its stadium. The competition starts with regional qualifying. Then it's on to the tournament, which is nationally televised. The interest rivals, or in some cases surpasses, the attention given to pro teams playing for championships.

Performances in the tournament sometimes are legendary and can push high school players to instant stardom. Such is the case of Daisuke Matsuzaka, who first became known in Japan through an amazing effort at Koshein. Matsuzaka pitched for Yokohama High School in 1998. The semifinal was played during a heat wave. Matsuzaka went all 17 innings of the legendary contest and threw 250 pitches. Yokohama won and advanced to the final.

But Matsuzaka wasn't done. He came back the next day to pitch for Yokohama in the tournament final. Not only did he win the game, but he pitched a no-hitter to give his team the national championship. It was no surprise, then, when Matsuzaka was selected first overall by the Seibu Lions in Japan's draft of young players. He had a great career in Japan, pitching in the Summer Olympics and the World Baseball Classic. Eventually the pitcher signed with the Boston Red Sox, where he won a World Series championship in 2007. Matsuzaka spent eight years in the United States and returned to pitch in Japan after the 2014 season.

Sadaharu Oh pitched four games in four days with severe blisters on his hand to lead his team to a title in the 1957 Koshien tournament. He wrote this in his autobiography:

> The press in our country makes much of "the spirit
> of high school baseball." And it is true—as far as it

goes. High school players back then—and now—give themselves to the game in ways that are both admirable and foolish. … The papers the next day and for some days following made much of the fact that I pitched with such an injury. It demonstrated this superb "spirit of high school baseball." But if the game had been lost—as well it might—the stories might have been different.

As for Ichiro, he led his team to the tournament in 1991, and Aikodai Medien did pull off some upsets in the early rounds. But Ichiro couldn't take his team all the way to the championship. Still, it was the first time the nation got a look at the skinny pitcher.

Sizing Up Ichiro

Based on high school statistics, Ichiro clearly was a top player. However, Japanese pro scouts, like their American counterparts, always will pick a good big player over a good smaller player. Ichiro at the end of high school was clearly one of the latter. He reportedly weighed about 120 pounds (54 kg). His body would fill out in the years to come, but early on, it was very difficult to project what sort of player he would become.

Maybe that's why he was not selected until the fourth and final round (thirty-sixth pick) of Japan's professional draft by the Orix BlueWave. Still, that selection meant he would be given a chance to play at his country's highest level. Suzuki had a chance to make a lifelong dream come true. He signed a contract with a bonus worth $43,000, well below his target figure.

Ichiro has been wearing the number 51 ever since his early years in professional baseball in Japan.

Ichiro Suzuki: A League of His Own

"I wanted to be a professional baseball player when I was kindergarten-age, but the moment that I realized it wasn't until the day I was drafted by the Orix," he said years later. "I really couldn't believe it until it happened. When I was in elementary school, the teacher said, 'Let's all have a reunion when you turn twenty years old.' I said, 'I won't be able to make it because I will be a professional baseball player.' Everyone laughed at me and joked about it, but it really ended up happening."

Chapter 2

Instant Success

The Orix BlueWave was a franchise that had a long history in Japanese professional baseball but not under that particular name.

The team was founded in 1936 by the Janshin Kyuko Railway Company, which eventually nicknamed the franchise the Hankyu Braves. It was one of the first pro teams in the country. The Braves are remembered today as the first Japanese team to sign African American players. They added such players as John Britton and Jimmy Newberry, who moved to the Far East when the Negro Leagues in America started to crumble, as more and more players began to integrate Major League Baseball.

The Braves made the Japan Series five times between 1967 and 1972 but lost to the Yomiuri Giants each time. For that achievement, manager Yukokio Nishimoto was called "the great manager in tragedy." But under a different manager, Toshiharu Ueda, Hankyu won three straight titles in the 1970s.

Opposite: Once Ichiro became a regular, he was an almost-instant star for Orix.

In October 1988, the franchise was sold to another company; the new owners switched the company name to the Orix Group in 1989. In 1989 and 1990, the team was called the Orix Braves. The franchise moved to Kobe in 1991 and became the Orix BlueWave. That's the team that drafted Ichiro in 1991.

Position Problem

Ichiro's first roadblock came right away, in his first training camp with the BlueWave. He had been drafted as a pitcher, but he wanted to play in the outfield. Shozo Doi, the manager of the BlueWave, took a look at Suzuki's swing and decided that the prospect should stick to pitching. It was an odd-looking swing, with spinning and lunging involved. Yet, it had worked for him so far.

Ichiro won the argument about playing the outfield, but he wasn't going to do it at the major league level immediately. Doi sent him to the minor leagues and gave batting instructor Kenichiro Kawamura a simple order: "Fix his swing."

Kawamura took a good look at Ichiro in the minors, and what he saw startled him. "I found his center of gravity was very strong," Kawamura said for a story for the *Seattle Times*. "He makes a perfect triangle with his body, which makes a perfect center of gravity. His head always sits on the top of the triangle. He looks like he goes forward, but he doesn't. It looked awkward, but when he hits the ball, it becomes the perfect form."

Even when Ichiro didn't hit the ball particularly well, he could beat out hits to the infield because he was so fast. Ichiro also still had a pitcher's arm. His throws from the outfield were strong and accurate. The BlueWave had itself a much better prospect than it first thought. Kawamura had Suzuki work on his legs to build up strength and predicted that he would become one of the best hitters in Japanese baseball within two years.

Ichiro went right to work, and he became one of the top hitters on his team. In fact, Suzuki's performance caught the eye of the BlueWave's management, and he was called up to the majors in June 1992. But it was too soon for Ichiro to take such a big step, and he showed he wasn't ready for it. He hit .253 in forty games, although he did get the first twenty-four hits of his career in the Japanese majors. Doi sent the young outfielder back to the minors with another order to change that unusual swing. Kawamura still refused. "I was so confident he would be a good batter if he gained his strength," he said. "He hadn't found his potential yet. I protected Ichiro. Going to the majors was too quick for him."

It was more of the same in 1993, as Doi and Kawamura still clashed. Ichiro had yet to show how good he could be at Japan's highest level. He took a step backward in another chance with the BlueWave, slumping to .188 in forty-three games. But the manager and the coach still didn't agree about Ichiro's style. When asked again to change Ichiro's swing, Kawamura said, "I would quit! I would quit! I would quit!"

There might have been a chance that we would never hear about Ichiro at that point, but fate played a role in his future. The BlueWave had a 70-56 record, but management fired Doi after the 1993 season. Doi, who had played fourteen seasons without hitting .300, never managed in Japanese baseball again.

The new manager was Akira Ogi, who had spent fourteen seasons playing infield for the Nishitetsu Lions. Ogi had an outgoing personality, unusual for Japanese baseball. He dressed in white suits and gold chains. Ogi had hit for an average of only .229 in his career,

Ichiro and his legendary manager with the BlueWave, Akira Ogi, enjoy a reunion in Seattle on August 15, 2004.

Ichiro Suzuki: A League of His Own

but he had five straight winning seasons to his credit as a manager in the Pacific League. Ogi wasn't willing to argue with Kawamura at the start of his new job. Ichiro, the word came, should keep his old swing.

This time, Ichiro was ready. He was now twenty years old, and his body had filled out somewhat. Ichiro was never going to be a classic power hitter, but he could hit the ball almost anywhere he wanted. The fun was about to begin.

Breakout Season

Ichiro took the Pacific League by storm in 1994. (Japanese baseball at its highest level is divided into two six-team leagues, the Pacific and the Central.) He piled up hits at an astonishing rate and showed some power as well as the ability to steal bases. While statistics aren't available, we can assume that opposing baserunners quickly learned not to try to take an extra base when the ball was hit to Ichiro. What's more, the BlueWave decided to promote him simply as Ichiro. That's a decision that has held up until this day.

Soon, the only question about Ichiro centered on how long he could continue to hit so well. His answer was to get on base at a record rate for the whole season. On September 14, 1994, he passed the Japanese record for hits in a season. The old mark was 191, set in 1950 by Tomio Fujimura of the Hanshin Tigers. A mere twelve days later, Ichiro became the first player in Japanese baseball history to reach 200 hits in a season. The game was stopped for a brief interview, and Ichiro simply told the crowd over the public address system, "I'll continue my efforts."

Ichiro finished the season with 210 hits in playing all 130 games for the BlueWave. The outfielder hit .385. The second-place finisher

Kenichiro Kawamura

Kenichiro Kawamura was an unlikely choice to become one of the most influential persons in Ichiro Suzuki's career.

Kawamura was a catcher for eleven seasons in Hankyu in the Japanese League (1972–1982). He had a career batting average of .267 and never hit .300 in a season. Kawamura never had more than 296 at-bats in a single season.

After retirement from playing the game, Kawamura became a hitting coach for the Orix BlueWave organization, and he saw Ichiro for the first time in 1992. The young outfielder had just been sent to the minors by the BlueWave, and manager Shozo Doi ordered Ichiro to change his swing. Les Carpenter of the *Guardian* wrote this about Kawamura's reaction to seeing the young player hit: "He knew he was watching brilliance when he saw Ichiro swing. And because Ichiro was very fast, he would get hits even when he didn't hit the ball well."

Ichiro thrived in Japan's minor league as a rookie, earning a trip to the BlueWave. He struggled there, and Doi still wanted the prospect to change his swing. Ichiro dug in his cleats and refused. "I was thinking, what if there was a different coach every year?" he said. "I'd have to change my style to suit each one of them. I wouldn't be playing very long if I did that."

Kawamura kept working with him, and Ichiro was ready when he joined the BlueWave for good at the age of twenty in 1994.

in the batting race, Ken Suzuki, hit .350, and no other regular on Ichiro's own team hit more than .307. He scored 111 runs, twice as many as any other player on the Orix roster. Ichiro's 41 doubles led the league, and his 13 homers were tied for the team lead. Add a total of 29 stolen bases, the Most Valuable Player award, an appearance on the end-of-the-season All-Star team, and a Gold Glove for fielding, and it's pretty clear that Ichiro had arrived. And he did it all for a salary that was about $80,000 when converted into US funds. The top salary in Major League Baseball that season was the $6.3 million paid to Bobby Bonilla.

It could be argued that Ichiro had his best all-around year in the Japanese league at the age of twenty. It also could be argued that Ichiro was just getting started—especially financially. His contract for 1995 was worth $2 million; no player in his league had ever earned so much at such a young age. The team could afford it: souvenir sales had gone up from $3 million to $13 million in 1994. Japan quickly fell in love with its new baseball superstar, and that meant he received a variety of endorsement opportunities.

As 1995 approached, Ichiro's new home of Kobe suffered the worst natural disaster in its history. An earthquake rocked the city, causing more than six thousand deaths. The team dedicated its season to the city, and Ichiro contributed large amounts of money to the relief effort. Then the BlueWave added a couple of ex-Oakland Athletics in Doug Jennings and Troy Neel. With Ichiro, Orix ran away with the championship of the Pacific League with an 82–47 record. By the way, the second-place team, the Chiba Lotte Marines, was managed by former American major league player and manager Bobby Valentine.

The BlueWave lost in Japan's equivalent of the World Series, but it was otherwise a fabulous year for Ichiro. He hit .342 to win the batting title by 29 points, pounded 25 homers, drove in 80 runs, and stole 49 bases in 58 attempts. He won his second MVP trophy.

Ichiro's father, Nobuyuki, certainly enjoyed his son's success, and he did it in a very public way. Nobuyuki often made the two-hour drive to see Ichiro's games in person. When he sat in the stands, he was often seen signing autographs for fans. Nobuyuki frequently gave interviews to reporters, and even wrote a book called *Musuko Ichiro* (My Son Ichiro). It helped turn Ichiro's childhood batting cage, the Airport Batting Center, into a tourist attraction.

Proving Their Worth

Ichiro certainly could look back at an outstanding season for himself and his team when 1995 was over. However, it seems pretty likely that he also was keeping track of what was taking place in American baseball. One of the biggest stories of the year took place in Los Angeles, as Japanese pitcher Hideo Nomo had jumped to the Dodgers.

Nomo had been an outstanding pitcher in the early 1990s. He joined the Osaka Kintetsu Buffaloes in 1990 at the age of twenty, and he became an instant star. Nomo had a record of 18–8 with an earned-run average of 2.91. The Buffaloes won only 67 games that season, and Nomo won eight more games than any other pitcher on the staff. He had similar statistics in 1991. In spring training of 1992, Nomo gave up a home run in an exhibition game to someone named Ichiro Suzuki, but went on to have one of his best seasons (18–8, 2.66). After another successful year in 1993, Nomo had won a total of 70 games in his four seasons as a top professional. **Tendinitis** allowed him to pitch for only 17 games in 1994, but he still had a

Hideo Nomo was a sensation when he arrived from Japan to pitch for the Los Angeles Dodgers in the 1990s.

winning record. Life was good for Nomo, who was earning a good salary in Japan.

However, he wanted more. An American agent named Arn Tellem found a **loophole** in the standard players' contract. The language was such that Japanese players who retired weren't prohibited from playing baseball for other teams outside of Japan. Nomo first announced his retirement from Japanese baseball at the age of twenty-six, which sparked the interest of several American teams. The Dodgers were at the front of the line for Nomo's services. They had to sweeten their offer for the pitcher, but eventually Nomo agreed to play for the Dodgers in 1995.

"There was just something about him," Dodger executive vice president Fred Claire told the *Los Angeles Times*. "Here's a guy who had everything in Japan. He had fame, fortune, a good life. He gave it all up just so he could pitch against the best. That impressed us. That impressed us a lot."

Even more impressive was Nomo's first-year performance with the Dodgers. He went 13–6 with a 2.54 earned-run average and led the league in strikeouts. Nomo won the Rookie of the Year award, was named to play in the All-Star Game, and finished fourth in the voting for the **Cy Young Award**. The first Japanese player to appear in an American major league game in almost thirty years had shown that the jump could be made. The question then became, would others follow?

"The most significant part is that for thirty years the Japanese didn't know how their players compared to ours," Dodgers manager Tom Lasorda told the *Los Angeles Times*. "What he's done has been a big boost to their baseball program. I guarantee, you, the next contracts they give out won't have that [retirement] loophole."

Lasorda was right; a "**Nomo clause**" soon was added to future Japanese contracts.

All-Star Performance

The 1996 season was even better for Ichiro for a couple of reasons. Most importantly, Orix took the last step and won a championship. He moved up to .356 with 193 hits, 84 RBIs and 34 stolen bases. That earned him a third-straight MVP trophy.

All that was memorable, naturally, but Ichiro also had a much different pleasant memory of that season. He became a pitcher, briefly. It was the 1996 All-Star Game, and the Pacific team was in command in the top of the ninth inning. Ichiro got the call to come in and end the game. The crowd was thrilled, of course, and roared as he retired the one batter he faced to end the game. The former high school pitcher now had performed the same task in one of the sport's biggest moments of the year.

Katsuya Nomura, manager of the Yakult Swallows, admired Ichiro from the opposing dugout: "He's wonderful. He hits well. He runs well. He plays good defense. He's polite in his private life and is kind to his parents. I've never seen anyone like him. It's strange that such a person is born into the world."

Another thrill was to come that year. After North America's major leagues had finished up their season, several top players crossed the Pacific to play in a series of exhibition games. The list of stars included Pedro Martinez, Barry Bonds, Cal Ripken Jr., Mike Piazza, and Alex Rodriguez. Piazza took a look at Ichiro in that series of games and said he was good enough to play at the top of the American baseball ladder. Ichiro modestly replied, "I could go, but I would probably be the bat boy." But later on he gave a more honest reaction: "I saw those MLB players and thought to myself, 'That's what I want to do.'"

The great seasons started to look like they had been produced by a copier. Ichiro never hit less than .342 in a full season in Japan. His **on-base percentage** was always above .400. His **slugging percentage** was always above .500. In 2000, Ichiro's OPS (on-base plus slugging percentage) was .999—the highest of his career.

Along the way, Ichiro became the top star in all of Japanese sports. His name became connected to several companies through endorsements. Mizuno, the sporting goods company, had signed Ichiro to a contract in 1995, and it worked out very well for both sides. But fame had an effect on his life outside of baseball. If Ichiro tried to sleep on one of Japan's famous bullet trains, fans would wake him and ask him for an autograph. Appearing in public became difficult.

It was no surprise, then, that when Ichiro found a woman that he wanted to marry, arrangements had to be very quiet. He married Yumiko Fukushima in 1999 in an unlikely place: Santa Monica, California. She was a sportscaster in Japan. Details about most of Ichiro's personal life remain hard to come by.

In 2000, Ichiro was twenty-six years old, which is considered close to the prime of a baseball player's life. He hit .387, a career high. That number was good for yet another batting title. In seven years as a regular, Ichiro had his league's best batting average seven times.

Ichiro Posted

At that point, Orix had a large problem on its hands. The BlueWave had just finished a sub-.500 season, and there wasn't great hope for the immediate future. What's more, Ichiro would finish his tenth

Ichiro's 1999 marriage to Yumiko Fukushima in San Diego, California, was huge news back in Japan.

season of Japanese baseball at the end of the 2001 season. That meant he would qualify for **free agency** and no doubt be paid more than the $5 million he was already earning. Orix, therefore, was likely to lose him to another team without any compensation.

The Japanese team decided to use the relatively new "posting system" for determining Ichiro's fate. An agreement between the American and Japanese leagues had been signed in 1998 in order to bring a little order to the process of a player's move from one to the other. Under this system, a team would designate a player for movement, and other teams would bid for the rights to negotiate a contract with that player. Therefore, the new team would have to pay for the right to sign the player, and then compensate the player as well.

Onix posted him in the fall of 2000. The next big step in Ichiro's career was about to take place.

Chapter 3

A Magical First Year

When word came that Ichiro Suzuki had the chance to come to North America to play baseball, all major league teams certainly paid attention. It was true that no Japanese non-pitcher had ever made a successful switch to Major League Baseball. However, Ichiro seemed like a good bet, considering his fabulous track record in Japan. Besides, it wouldn't cost a major league team any talent to acquire Ichiro—only money. That was attractive.

While all of the teams were free to bid, there was one that figured to be the front-runner: the Seattle Mariners. First of all, Nintendo—the Japanese video game manufacturer—owned the Mariners at the time. Second, Seattle was something of an American gateway to the Far East, and thus offered comforts to an incoming player that wouldn't be present in, say, Pittsburgh. Third, the Mariners already had a Japanese player on their major-league roster. Kazuhiro Sasaki had arrived in 2000 at the age of 32 and had 37 saves for Seattle. Sasaki was said to be a good friend of Ichiro.

Opposite: The outfielder couldn't go anywhere on a field without being followed by cameras, many from publications in Japan.

That all may have scared off some potential teams. The Boston Red Sox were said to be interested in Ichiro, but one of their scouts said they expected the Mariners to outbid everyone for the outfielder. The words of Ichiro's agent, Tony Attanasio, may have played a role in the process too. "I talked to ten teams," Attanasio told the *New York Times*. "I might have dissuaded some by telling them, 'If you don't have a strong Japanese influence in your community, don't bid because it's not going to work.'"

When money is the only ingredient for adding talent, the teams from New York City and their deep pockets usually come up in the conversation. The Yankees didn't have a great need for an outfielder. They were coming off their third straight World Series championship and had a fine player in right field in Paul O'Neill. An expensive new player might cause problems for the team's salary structure as well.

The New York Mets made more sense. Bobby Valentine had managed that team to the 2000 World Series (where they lost to the Yankees), and he was one of Ichiro's biggest boosters—having seen firsthand what the outfielder did in Japan while managing there. In addition, the Mets' outfield in 2000 consisted of Benny Agbayani, Jay Payton, and Derek Bell. Ichiro would have been a good fit.

Naturally, the Los Angeles Dodgers also came up in any discussion about signing Ichiro. The Dodgers had benefited from the success of Hideo Nomo in the late 1990s, so they saw that a Japanese player could succeed in the right environment. They had a couple of good outfielders in Gary Sheffield and Shawn Green, but they were missing a regular center fielder. Maybe Ichiro could be part of the puzzle. The Angels also reportedly had shown an interest in him. However, there wasn't an obvious spot in the starting lineup for him, so it didn't seem as if Anaheim—as the team was called at the time—would be a strong bidder.

Mariners Win Bid

When the bids were opened on November 10, 2000, the Mariners had offered $13,125,000 for the chance to sign Ichiro. That was the winning bid. According to reports, the Mets, Dodgers, and Angels didn't come close to winning the auction.

"I anticipated there were going to be some teams that extended beyond us," Mets general manager Steve Phillips said after the announcement had been made. "Most teams expected Seattle would be aggressive."

The Mets later signed another Japanese outfielder for their roster for the 2001 season. Tsuyoshi Shinjo played in 123 games for the Mets in 2001, hitting .268. He joined the San Francisco Giants a year later, and that fall he became the first Japanese player to take part in the World Series.

The Mariners' offer was accepted by the BlueWave, giving Seattle thirty days to sign Ichiro to a contract. It took only nine days for the two sides to agree to a three-year deal. Reports later said that Ichiro received a total of $27 million over the course of those three years. "I'm confident, or I wouldn't be sitting here right now," the new Mariner said at the time. Howard Lincoln, Seattle's top executive, added, "The Mariners recognize that Ichiro is one of the very best baseball players in the world. He has tremendous talent and will fit nicely with our team and organization."

There had been uncertainty about the Mariners entering the 2001 season. They had been a playoff team in 2000, losing to the New York Yankees in the American League Championship Series. However, they had lost their biggest star, Alex Rodriguez. The shortstop, who after seven seasons in the majors was already being compared to the all-time greats, had left as a free agent to join the

Texas Rangers for a reported $252 million contract. He took his .316 batting average, 41 home runs and 132 runs batted in from the 2000 season with him. That was a huge hole in the lineup to replace. Ichiro wasn't going to supply that sort of power for the Mariners, but the team hoped he'd add all of his skills to the team that had come close to playing in the World Series the year before. The new outfielder knew he'd face the biggest test of his career, and he added 20 pounds (9 kg) of muscle in the offseason to help him in his new surroundings.

Story of Spring

Naturally, Ichiro was the biggest story surrounding the Mariners when they arrived in Arizona for spring training. There had never been an everyday player (in other words, a non-pitcher) from Japan who had earned a starting job in North America, and there was some degree of skepticism from many. That included the Seattle manager, Lou Piniella, as well as some of Ichiro's teammates. "I think everyone was skeptical," pitcher Jeff Nelson said. "He didn't really do anything in spring training, and people were thinking, 'This guy might be overmatched.'"

Part of the problem is that most people had never seen Ichiro play. He had taken part in the Mariners' spring training in 1999 as part of a visit by his Japanese team, but food poisoning prevented him from displaying his talents fully. When Ichiro kept hitting weak grounders to left field during Seattle's 2001 training camp, that concern grew.

Finally, Piniella said to Ichiro one day, "Ichiro, do you ever turn on the ball?" Ichiro said he did at times. Turning on a ball allows a player to pull a hit to his strong side, in the left-handed Ichiro's case

Manager Lou Piniella, once a good hitter himself, quickly learned that Ichiro could do almost anything with a baseball bat.

to right field, and sometimes pull it with power. Then, in his first at-bat of an exhibition game, he pulled the ball to right field, over the fence and up a hill. Ichiro came back to the dugout and said to Piniella, "Is that turning on the ball, Skip?" Piniella remembers telling his new outfielder, "You can do whatever you want the rest of the year." Ichiro went on to hit .321 in spring training games.

The veteran manager, who had won a World Series championship with the Cincinnati Reds in 1990, put Ichiro in the leadoff spot in his batting order right away. It didn't take Ichiro long to make an impact. He picked up two hits in his very first game as a Mariner—both of them up the middle. That earned him a kiss on the cheek from Piniella, which left Ichiro a little embarrassed. "I thought maybe every time we won, and every time I did well, he was going to give me a kiss," he said.

Only four days later, the outfielder's first major-league homer arrived in a dramatic way. With the score tied, 7-7, in the top of the tenth inning, Ichiro's two-run homer gave Seattle the win over Rodriguez's new team in Texas.

Showing Off His Arm

However, his biggest early impression might have been made by his throwing arm. Ichiro and the Mariners were in Oakland, and the fans there had been taunting and booing the newcomer. In the top of the eighth, Ichiro hit a pinch-hit single to put his team in front. He stayed in the game and took over in right field. The Athletics threatened in the bottom of the inning, with Terrence Long on first. Ramon Hernandez singled to right, and Long rounded second and took off for third. Ichiro threw the ball to third baseman David Bell on a line. Bell barely had to move to tag out Long.

Reaction came swiftly. "It was going to take a perfect throw to get me—and that's what he did," Long said. "I'll tell you what, you could hang a lot of clothes on that throw," Piniella said. The throw is still preserved on YouTube to show everyone what had happened. It didn't take long for word to get around: don't run on Ichiro's arm.

Ichiro and the Mariners set the tone for a fabulous start. Seattle went 20–5 in the month of April, destroying almost everything in their way. They had a nine-game lead over the rest of the American League's West Division. After a battering of the Rangers in a series, Rodriguez predicted that the Mariners might win 115 games. Ichiro had hits in 23 of those 25 games, hitting .336 along the way. He was named Rookie of the Month. Ichiro had back-to-back games with a single, a double, and a triple. For someone playing in a new league in a new country with strange food and customs, the newcomer was adjusting quite well to his new surroundings.

Ichiro made a little history when he faced Angels reliever Shigetoshi Hasegawa; it was the first time an Asian-born pitcher faced an Asian-born everyday player. He singled on the first pitch of the at-bat. Speaking of history, another Japanese pitcher, Hideo Nomo, reached a landmark that April as well. Pitching for the Boston Red Sox, Nomo threw his second career no-hitter.

Japanese players were clearly having an impact on Major League Baseball, and most assumed that more of them would be arriving in the near future. "There are guys over there who can not only play in our league but can also be a big part of it, and you're going to see more and more," Angels manager Mike Scioscia told *Sports Illustrated*. "These guys are going to make their mark in the majors."

April was the best month of the Mariners' season, but it wasn't out of the ordinary. There wasn't a month that season that the team didn't win at least two-thirds of its games. Bret Boone, a good player picked up from San Diego in the offseason, was a great player in 2001. He usually hit fifth in the lineup, and someone was usually on base when he got to the plate. The RBIs mounted up throughout the summer. Edgar Martinez was still one of the league's best designated hitters at the age of thirty-eight, and he pounded out hits. First baseman John Olerud and outfielder Mike Cameron were having fine years. The list of starting pitchers was deep, even if it didn't have a standout at the top of the rotation. **Closer** Sasaki was always ready to provide a happy ending for the Mariners in his role as one of the best relief pitchers in the game. The bench was filled with role players who could contribute to the team's success.

Still, Ichiro was frequently the center of attention. In mid-May, he was leading the league in hits and stolen bases and carrying a .365 batting average. Ichiro already had put together hitting streaks of fifteen and twenty-three games. "He's a legitimate hitter, no question," Yankees manager Joe Torre told *Sports Illustrated.* "I don't think you can pitch him one way. You can go in and out, up and down, and he makes the adjustment. You can get ahead in the count, and Suzuki still seems relaxed. He doesn't seem to have any weaknesses."

Mariners Marching

The Mariners went on a fifteen-game winning streak that started at the end of May, and it became rather obvious that no team was going to stop them from winning the division title. The team's dominance was on display that summer when the annual All-Star Game was played in Seattle, by coincidence. That game is mostly remembered for a position switch just before the top of the first inning.

The Mariners were well-represented in the 2001 All-Star Game; Kazuhiro Sasaki of the Mariners earned the save.

A Magical First Year

Ichiro Suzuki: A League of His Own

Jay Buhner

It should be more than a footnote that the Seattle Mariners had a regular right fielder before Ichiro Suzuki arrived on the team. What's more, he was a very good player, and a popular one.

Jay Buhner came to the Mariners in a trade with the Yankees that saw New York receive Ken Phelps. It's considered one of the worst trades in Yankee history. Phelps had been a good power hitter for the Mariners, while Buhner was an unproven prospect. Upon switching uniforms, Phelps's career slid downhill, while Buhner became a big part of a Mariners team that featured such players as Ken Griffey Jr. and Alex Rodriguez.

It took until 1991 for Buhner to win a regular job, but he hit twenty-seven homers that year. Buhner hit at least twenty homers in the next three seasons as well, then really picked up his level of play. The outfielder had forty or more home runs in 1995, 1996, and 1997. That 1995 team just missed reaching the World Series.

But Buhner was hurt for much of 1998 and 1999. He came back in 2000 to hit twenty-six homers but tore the arch in his foot in spring training of 2001 and missed much of that season. He retired at the end of the year.

Buhner was a big, bald Texan who seemed to hit a homer or strike out at each at-bat. In other words, he couldn't have been more different from the man who replaced him.

Opposite: Jay Buhner was a distinctive figure on the baseball diamond during a productive stay with the Mariners.

Rodriguez, the starting shortstop for the American League, moved to third base so that Cal Ripken Jr., in his final year of a great career, could return to his original position of shortstop for a few innings. Ripken later homered to cap a memorable night for the Baltimore Orioles' legend.

Once the actual game started, Ichiro—who led all players in the voting for the starting lineup with 3.3 million ballots—and his seven Seattle teammates took center stage. He wasted no time showing a national audience just what he could do. He hit a single in the bottom of the first inning off future Hall of Famer Randy Johnson, and then stole second base. Sasaki closed out the game, and the American League had a 4–1 victory.

Seattle loved its new star. It didn't take long for Ichiro to be mobbed by fans when he tried to walk down the street. Fans packed Safeco Field and chanted his name. A little boy held up a sign that read, "I want to be Ichiro when I grow up." University of Washington professor Shawn Wong summarized Ichiro's effect on the city in an article for the *Seattle Times*: "I'm beginning to think that an entire city can understand how race changes their culture and society and can embrace and even encourage that change."

While Ichiro was changing minds and attracting fans in North America, he was achieving unmatched popularity in Japan. Mariners games were shown on Japanese television—once live, once on tape. Fans had the chance to see Ichiro do knee-bends in the outfield and stretch while waiting to hit. Ichiro's previous at-bats were replayed constantly. The All-Star Game was shown live in Japan as well. Taxi drivers in Tokyo listened to Mariners' games while working.

Drawing Attention

The coverage of Ichiro by Japanese newspapers was overwhelming and amazing. A total of forty-seven journalists spent that entire season covering Ichiro—not all of American baseball, not the Mariners, but Ichiro. The reporters traveled all across the country for the entire season in order to chronicle the outfielder's exploits for readers who were anxious to find out about every possible detail.

It couldn't have been easy to have forty-seven journalists following you around day after day, and Ichiro limited their access. He allowed only one Japanese reporter to ask questions after each game. By all accounts, his answers were short and not at all interesting. Ichiro even cut off that amount of access for a while after a photographer was in the way when the baseball player tried to back out of a driveway. But a truce was soon reached, and the Japanese reporters were back to searching for the few available crumbs of information. When Piniella had a news conference, he could count on three or four questions about Ichiro from the pack of reporters—every day.

The 2001 season moved into the second half, and nothing changed for the Mariners. The season was barely half over when baseball observers had come to some conclusions. Alfonso Soriano of the Yankees may have been the favorite back in March for rookie of the year honors, but that trophy could have been awarded to Ichiro by August 1.

Even one of the greatest one-game collapses in Seattle's franchise history couldn't slow them for long. On August 5 in Cleveland, the Mariners had a 12–0 lead on the Indians, which later became a 14–2

The amount of attention Ichiro received from the Japanese media during his first spring training was astounding.

Ichiro Suzuki: A League of His Own

A Magical First Year

margin after six innings. But Cleveland scored three runs in the seventh, four in the eighth, and five in the ninth to tie the game, 14–14. The Indians won the game, 15–14, in 11 innings. The Mariners shrugged it off and won seven of their next nine games. Along the way, Ichiro kept pounding out hits.

In mid-September, the Mariners wrapped up the American League West title. The team had to wait a week because the sport shut down for seven days after the terrorist attacks on the United States on September 11. The celebration over a division title was muted and respectful. From there, the only question left about the Mariners' regular season centered on whether they could break the major league record for wins in a season. The mark was 116, set by the 1906 Chicago Cubs in a 154-game season.

The Mariners gave it a try, winning 10 of 11 after a four-game losing streak. That got them to 116 to tie the mark, but they lost to the Rangers on the season's final day. A 116–46 record would have to do. It was still the best winning percentage (.716) in baseball since 1961, when the sport switched to a 162-game season. The New York Yankees had won 114 games in 1998. Those Mariners' wins were good for a ticket to the postseason playoffs, period. While the best team usually emerges over the course of a long season, there are no guarantees in a playoff series.

The first round matched the Mariners against the Cleveland Indians, who had such talented players as Roberto Alomar and Jim Thome. The Indians gave the Mariners fits in the best-of-five series. Bartolo Colon set the tone for Cleveland with eight shutout innings in a 5–0 win. The Indians also won Game Three by a 17–2 count, so the Mariners had to win two straight games in order to survive. They did exactly that. In Game Four, Seattle trailed, 1–0, after six innings but rallied for a 6–2 win. Then in Game Five in Seattle, the Mariners' pitchers limited Cleveland to four hits in a 3–1 win.

Ichiro handled the pressures of playoff baseball in America quite well. He hit .600 for the series, scored four runs, and drove in three more. The hits included a huge single in Game Four off of Colon that gave the Mariners the lead for good. "I was sitting next to (John) Olerud when Ichiro got the hit," catcher Tom Lampkin said. "I kept saying to John, 'How does he do it?' I don't even know if he's aware that guys are on base. His ability to stay on an even keel is amazing. I've never seen anything like it."

And in Game Five, when every pitch was crucial, Ichiro went 3 for 4. "It's very simple," outfielder Mike Cameron said. "Time and time again, Ichiro has been our go-to guy. He hits, we win."

Disappointing Finish

It was on to the American League Championship Series, and the Yankees were waiting for them. New York had won 95 games in the regular season, 21 fewer than the Mariners. But they had won the last three World Series championships and four of the last five. The Yankees had lost the first two games of their best-of-five first-round series against the Oakland Athletics, but shortstop Derek Jeter's famous "flip" to catcher Jorge Posada late in Game Three preserved a 1–0 victory for New York, and the Yankees won Games Four and Five to advance.

The Yankees continued their roll by winning the first two games of the series in Seattle. The Mariners could only generate a pair of runs in each of those games. Ichiro had a hit in each of the contests. In Yankee Stadium, the Mariners' bats warmed up in a 14–3 romp; Bret Boone drove in five runs, and Ichiro had a hit. But Seattle's

The two men who were both the Most Valuable Player and Rookie of the Year in the same year, Ichiro and Fred Lynn, exchange memories in San Diego.

Ichiro Suzuki: A League of His Own

offense disappeared in Game Four, getting only two hits in a loss. Game Five was no contest. New York had a 9–0 lead after six innings. The Yankees finished with a 12–3 score.

Just like that, the Mariners' magical season was over. Ichiro had hit only .222 in the series with the Yankees, but he wasn't alone. The entire Seattle team hit .211, and that included a 15-hit performance in Game Three. The history books aren't particularly kind to that group of Mariners. If you look at the list of the teams that won the most regular season games in a year, Seattle is the only team that didn't make the World Series. The Mariners are grouped with the 1906 Cubs (116 wins) and 1954 Indians (111 wins) as teams that couldn't win a championship after great regular seasons.

Still, it had been a remarkable year—especially for Ichiro. His regular-season statistics were amazing. The outfielder led the league in at-bats (692), hits (242), stolen bases (56), and batting average (.350). The hit total was the most by a rookie in major-league history.

Earning Recognition

The honors started coming in shortly after the Arizona Diamondbacks had defeated the Yankees in a memorable World Series. Ichiro received all but one of the votes for the American League Rookie of the Year award. Ichiro said that he was a "little embarrassed" to win the rookie honors, because he had played for several years in Japan's top league. By any definition, though, the newcomer to American play had one of the greatest rookie seasons in baseball history. In addition, Ichiro picked up a Gold Glove as the league's best fielder at his position, and a Silver Slugger trophy as one of the top hitters among outfielders.

A week later came the news about the results of the voting for the Most Valuable Player trophy—one of the closest elections in the sport's history. Ichiro won that trophy too, edging out Jason Giambi of the Athletics by eight points. The Mariners' outfielder had eleven first-place votes to Giambi's eight. A case could be made that Giambi's season was better—he hit .342 with 38 homers and 120 RBIs—but Ichiro clearly belonged in the argument.

With that award, Ichiro had made baseball history. He was only the second player ever to win a Rookie of the Year trophy and a Most Valuable Player award in the same season. Fred Lynn did it for the Boston Red Sox in 1975. "I am very pleased and honored to be among those players to be called candidates of the AL MVP this year," Ichiro said after winning the MVP honor. "I did not imagine myself to be at the top of the list."

When reminded that he'd be forever linked with the greatest players in the history of the game, he replied, "To be among those legendary great players, I cannot be a regular ordinary player any more. I have to be a player exciting to both teammates and opponents."

Ichiro was the only person who thought he was an "ordinary player."

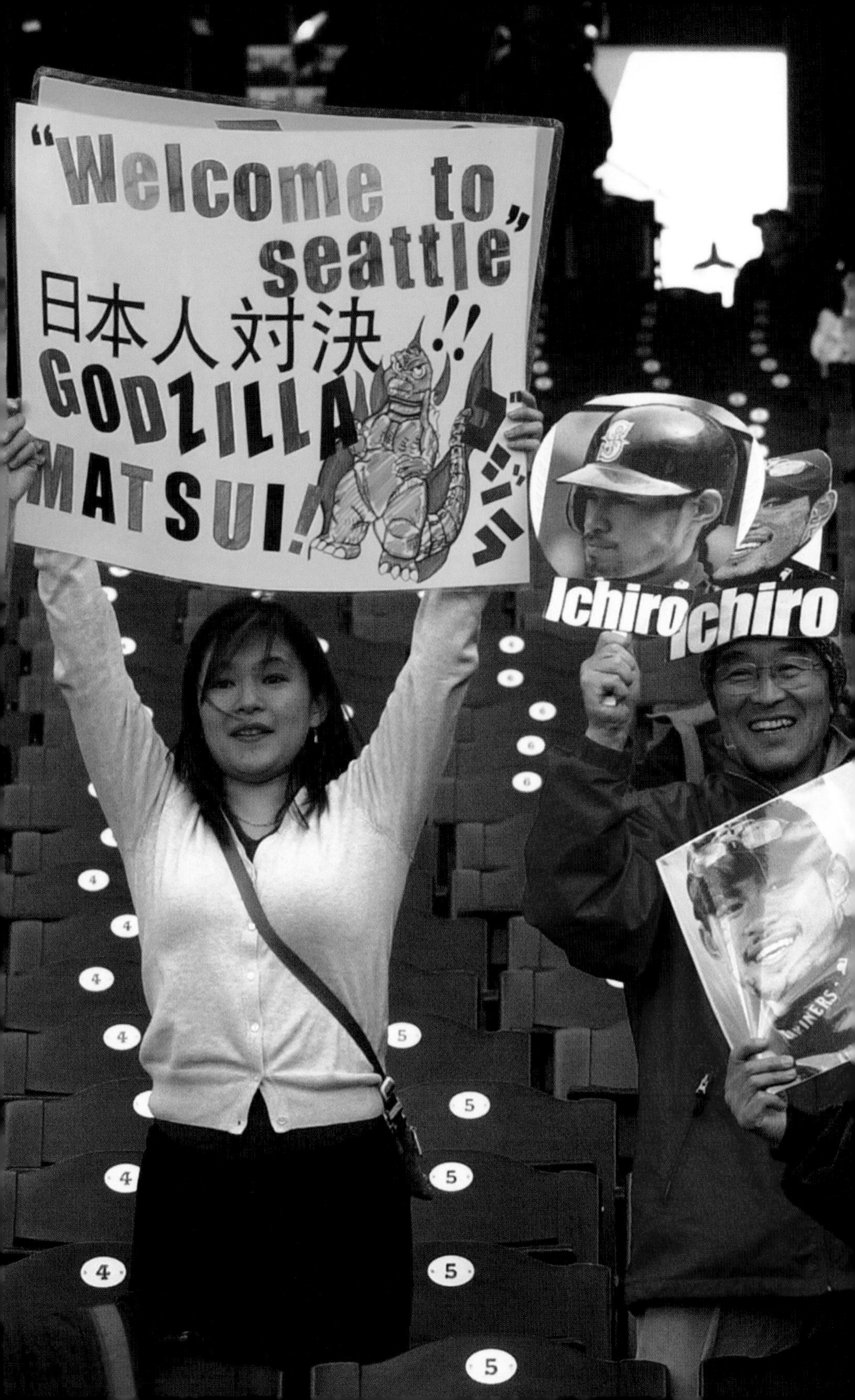
"Welcome to" seattle
日本人対決!!
GODZILLA
MATSUI!
Ichiro
Ichiro

Chapter 4

An Established Star

As Ichiro became ready to take part in his second full season in North America, many on this side of the Atlantic wondered what he would do next. A Most Valuable Player trophy was a difficult act to follow, and it had taken Ichiro no time at all to become one of the best players in the major leagues.

Many had predicted when Ichiro joined the Mariners that he might need some time to become comfortable in the United States. The adjustments now would be fewer in number, and he could relax knowing that he could compete in Major League Baseball. Therefore, with one year in the United States under his belt, he could be even better. On the other hand, Ichiro had been twenty-seven during his fabulous first season in Seattle. That's the age when many players reach their peak. Some thought, then, the 2001 season might be the high point of his career.

The questions were more profound in Japan. The Japanese had seen one of their own leave their country and achieve great success in North America as an everyday player for the first time in history.

Opposite: A visit by Hideki Matsui and the Yankees gave Japanese American baseball fans in Seattle two reasons to cheer.

The successful move had taken Ichiro's celebrity to a new level in Japan, as he was almost ever-present in newscasts and commercials. This was no small achievement for someone who spent a majority of his time half a world away.

What's more, Japanese teams could never match the salaries paid by major league teams. Ichiro probably would stay on the other side of the Pacific for as long as he was a contributor. No matter how much national pride was involved, Ichiro's success could be considered a bit of bad news for Japanese baseball. Would top players now automatically head to Major League Baseball in search of fame and fortune? Would Japan's leagues simply be in the business of supplying its best players to North America?

"Every day, people [in Japan] are watching major league baseball games, and short term, that's not so good for us," said Steve Inow, the general manager of Orix when Ichiro's contract rights were sold to Seattle. "These are difficult times. Japanese baseball is at a turning point. Which way do we go?"

In 2002, Kaz Matsui's reaction of Ichiro's success was rather typical. "When I think about him being in the major leagues, it amazes me," he told *Sports Illustrated*. "Then I see Ichiro getting two, three hits a game? I get so much out of it." Matsui was in the middle of a streak of seven straight seasons of hitting .300 in Japanese baseball when he made those remarks. The second baseman signed with the New York Mets in 2004.

Magic Wand

Ichiro started the 2002 season quite well for the Mariners. His batting average was above .360 in June, and he was continuing to be an absolute master with the bat. "Sometimes he makes the bat look like a magic wand," Seattle third base coach John McLaren told *USA Today*. "He's a unique hitter. I think he studies the defense. He has such bat control that he can put it where he wants."

In fact, some pitchers almost sounded resigned to the fact that Ichiro could defeat them no matter what they did. "I wouldn't try to do too much because it's a waste of time," said Mariners reliever Shigetoshi Hasegawa. "If I had to face him with runners at first and second, I'd have to think about it. But in the first inning or third inning, who cares? Don't try to do too much, throw twenty pitches and end up giving up a ground-ball base hit. Just throw him a fastball, maybe down and away."

Ichiro had become a gate attraction by this point in North America, a magnet especially for Japanese Americans. Yuka Yonashiro drove more than three hours one day from Toledo, Ohio, to Cincinnati to watch Ichiro and the Mariners play the Reds. "I just want to watch him," she said. "I expect that he'll have a hit, make a steal."

After a strong first half of the season, Ichiro slumped somewhat. His batting average dropped a bit. The outfielder finished with "only" 208 hits (200 hits is considered a statistical benchmark), good for a .321 batting average. Interestingly, he led the American League in intentional walks with 27; that is a statistic usually dominated by power hitters. It wasn't a great season, but it was a very good one.

Ichiro had a total of 450 hits in his first two major-league seasons, the most in history, and he was the sixth player in history to reach 200 hits in each of his first two years. Meanwhile, the team was still good—just not as good. The Mariners won 93 games, a drop of 23 from the previous season. They had slumped as a team when Ichiro did. The Mariners finished third in the division, and they started to look old. Six of their nine starters were at least thirty-two years old.

The 2003 season for Ichiro and the Mariners was close to a duplicate of 2002. The outfielder's batting average dropped to .312, but he still picked up 212 hits. That made Ichiro the first player in baseball history to have 200 or more hits in his first three seasons. He again was the leading vote-getter for the All-Star Team, the third straight time that had happened. As for the Mariners, they had the exact same record in 2003 as they did in 2002—93–69—even if they moved up a notch from third place to second. They weren't getting any younger, with only one starter under the age of twenty-nine (Carlos Guillen, twenty-seven). Ichiro would turn thirty at the end of that season.

Good Company

A highlight of the season came in the first month. Hideki Matsui had signed with the New York Yankees in the offseason, and he and Ichiro were to play against each other in Major League Baseball for the first time on April 30. Matsui was one of the great power hitters in the history of Japanese baseball, and he decided he, like Ichiro, needed the challenge of playing at a higher level of competition.

"None of the Japanese players who hit the longball have come over here," Ichiro said. "I am in awe of his determination to play here. He has a brave mind to come over here. I don't know him personally but what I heard about him is that his attitude toward baseball is great and sincere, so I hope he can have great years in coming years. But at the same time, looking at him as a Mariner—the Yankees are a tough team to beat, and we always want to beat him. So I don't want

Hideki Matsui followed Ichiro across the Pacific Ocean, and had a productive career in North America.

him to be successful (when we play) because we want to beat him."

Matsui's team won that first game, 8–5, and he did better in the game with a 1 for 4 performance and a run batted in. Ichiro went 0 for 5. There would be many more matchups in the future.

By the end of the 2003 season, Ichiro's original contract had expired. It put him in a position to make a lot of money. He could certainly stay with the Mariners, who wanted him back. But he was free to go back to Japan and play if he so desired. A four-year, $44 million offer from Seattle may have played a part in his decision, as he signed to stay with the team through 2007.

Ichiro's return was some good news for a team that was struggling. The Mariners of 2001 were becoming a distant memory rather quickly. The nine players who had the most at-bats in the Seattle lineup in 2004 were all thirty or over. Ichiro was one of the youngsters at thirty, along with Randy Winn. A thirty-five-year-old Bret Boone saw his production decline; he'd be traded and out of baseball at the end of 2005. Designated hitter Edgar Martinez had his worst season since breaking into the majors in 1989. He might not have known it, but he was playing the last season of a career that might get him into the Hall of Fame.

As for the pitching, the Mariner staff had an ugly season. A relief pitcher named Ron Villone led the team in wins with eight. No starter had more than seven wins. Jamie Moyer went from 21–7 in 2003 to 7–13. Ryan Franklin dropped from 11–13 to 4–16. The team won 63 games against 99 losses—a 53-game drop in wins from 2001.

There was only one constant: Ichiro. Even he started out slowly, hitting .255 at the end of April. He fit right in with the rest of the Mariners. But then the outfielder warmed up. He piled up 50 hits in May, hitting .400 in the process. After a so-so June, Ichiro had more than 50 hits in both July and August—with accompanying batting averages of .432 and .463 respectively. On the morning of September 1, Ichiro found himself with 212 hits for a batting average of .371.

Record in Sight

Suddenly, the name of George Sisler started to pop up in baseball circles again.

Sisler was a Hall of Famer, but by 2004 few people remembered seeing him, or even his sons Dave and Dick, play. He had played from 1915 until 1930, hitting .400 twice. But baseball is a sport that loves its records, and Sisler had one of the more durable ones in the record book. He piled up 257 hits in 1920, and that was still the major league record eighty-four years later. Only a few records were older, and they were relics of a very different game. For example, Jack Chesbro of the New York Highlanders (the predecessors of the Yankees) won 41 games in the 1904 season. That one appears to be unbreakable in the modern era as most pitchers don't even get to make 41 starts.

But Ichiro had a chance to make history. When asked in August about the possibility of catching Sisler, Ichiro replied, "I'm not a big guy, and hopefully kids could look at me and see that I'm not muscular and not physically imposing, that I'm just a regular guy. So if somebody with a regular body can get into the record books, kids can look at that. That would make me happy."

He needed 45 hits in the final weeks of the season to reach Sisler's mark. After three months of having 50 or more hits, Ichiro figured to have a chance. The leadoff man started September

After Ichiro broke George Sisler's record for hits in a season, set in 1920, he saluted Sisler's daughter, Frances Sisler Drochelman.

Ichiro Suzuki: A League of His Own

with hits in eight straight games, including a 5-for-5 performance against the White Sox on September 4. After a small slump in mid-September, Ichiro got back on track with five hits against the Angels on September 21. It was part of an eleven-game hitting streak. When September was over, Ichiro was at 256 hits—one back of Sisler's mark, with three games to break it.

The eighty-four-year wait was about to end. Ichiro led off the bottom of the first at Seattle's Safeco Field with a chopper over the head of Texas third baseman Hank Blalock to tie the mark. Then in the third, the outfielder drove a 3-2 pitch up the middle for a hit, and the quest was over. David Andriesen of the *Seattle Post-Intelligencer* described the scene this way:

> The sellout crowd went wild after the record-breaking hit, fireworks exploded and the theme from *The Natural* bellowed. The game was halted for several minutes as the Mariners dugout emptied, players smothering a grinning Ichiro with hugs. He trotted about 50 feet to the front-row seats where five members of Sisler's family, including his 81-year-old daughter, Frances Sisler Drochelman, were standing and applauding.

Just to make sure, Ichiro added his third hit of the night in the sixth inning. He also had a total of three more hits in the next two games to finish at 262.

The record was simply another way of showing what a unique and superb player he was, no matter where he was from. Bruce Jenkins of the *San Francisco Chronicle* put it this way in 2004:

Fact Checking

The Mariners' statistical department was busy compiling facts about Ichiro's 2004 season. Here is what it came up with:

- Had 924 hits in his major league career after four years. No one had ever had so many over any four-year span.
- Led the league in hits by 46, the largest such margin in baseball history.
- Hit .372 to win his second batting title.
- Had 225 singles, and 57 infield hits.
- Went eight for eight in one stretch of games on Sept. 21–22.
- Became the fifth player in history to have four five-hit games in a season.

There's nobody like Ichiro in either league—now or ever. He exists strictly within his own world, playing a game 100 percent unfamiliar to everyone else. The game has known plenty of 'slap' hitters, but none who sacrifice so much natural ability for the sake of the art. … The man lives for hits, little tiny ones, and the glory of standing atop the world in that category. Every spring, scouts or media types write him off, swearing that opposing pitchers have found the key, and they are embarrassingly wrong.

Through four seasons, Ichiro had been an All-Star four times and

Ichiro Suzuki: A League of His Own

a Gold Glover four times. In 2005, he showed off those skills with his glove in what might have been the best catch of his career.

Garrett Anderson of the Angels hit a deep blast to right field in a May game in Seattle. Ichiro went back, back, back, and then ran into the wall. That wasn't a problem. He simply dug his foot into the wall, pulled himself up by grabbing the top of the wall, adjusted for the flight of the ball, made the catch, and plopped back down on to the field. Even Ichiro was thrilled by the play.

"I imagined the ball to be (hit) a little farther than it was," he said. "When I got up there, it looked like a basketball. I've imagined it so many times."

Most of his opponents were very impressed. "I don't think people realize how hard a catch that was," Angels outfielder Steve Finley said. "He just ran to a spot. He never even looked at the ball. He jumped on the wall, turned, and the ball was right there. Not too many outfielders can do that." Manager Mike Scioscia added, "I don't know if I've ever seen a better catch. Incredible … You could sense that was something special as soon as it happened."

In spite of the catch that thrilled the 21,184 in Safeco Field, the Mariners lost, 5–0. That was typical. Seattle never got more than a game above .500 (more wins than losses) throughout the season, sinking to 69–93 by the end of the year. That was 10 games behind anyone else in the American League West. The Mariners had picked up a couple of good hitters in Richie Sexton and Adrian Beltre, but the pitching staff was still weak. Japanese native Shigetoshi Hasegawa completed his time in the major leagues; he left the Mariners at the end of the 2005 season.

As for Ichiro, he had a good season for most players but not for him. He hit a career-low .303 but still piled up 206 hits. The

Ichiro, manager Sadaharu Oh, and the rest of the Japanese team took home the gold medal for winning the World Baseball Classic in 2006.

outfielder also had the 1,000th hit of his career, becoming the third-fastest player in terms of games played to reach that milestone.

The 2006 season brought a new event to the baseball calendar: The World Baseball Classic (WBC). The idea was to bring sixteen national teams together for a preseason competition. It was the first professional event of its kind, and a chance for Ichiro to play with others of Japanese origin in a meaningful way. Japan survived the first two rounds along with South Korea, the Dominican Republic and Cuba. The United States was eliminated by a tiebreaker.

In the semifinals, Ichiro went 3 for 5 to help Japan knock off South Korea. Koji Uehara, who later had success in Major League Baseball, threw seven scoreless innings to earn the win. In the championship final, Japan beat Cuba, 10–6. Daisuke Matsuzaka was the tournament MVP. He jumped to the Boston Red Sox a year later and helped that team win a World Series. Ichiro went 2 for 4 and scored three runs.

"Apart from the Olympics, I really wanted this WBC tournament to be the event that decides the true world champions, so that's why I participated in this event," Ichiro said. "And at the end, I was able to be on the championship team, and this is probably the biggest moment of my baseball career."

The performance launched him into one of his best seasons. Ichiro hit .351 with 238 hits in 2007, and his 68 RBIs were one short of his career high of 69 set in 2001. At the All-Star Game, Ichiro hit the first inside-the-park home run in the contest's history and was awarded the game's Most Valuable Player trophy at its conclusion. It was the first such homer of his long career. "I thought it was going to

Quotes about Ichiro Suzuki

"The game is just different for this man. He sees spaces on the field and guides the ball where he wants it to go, just like he's playing slow-pitch softball."
—Twins Manager and Hall of Fame Player Paul Molitor

"I wish you could put a camera at third base to see how he hits the ball and see the way it deceives you. You can call some guys' infield hits cheap, but not his. He has amazing technique."
—Brandon Inge of the Tigers

"I love the guy. He's cool. He's got a cool hairstyle. Cool clothes. Cool car. Besides, anybody that just goes by one name has got to be cool. Man, he's Ichiro. That says it all, doesn't it?"
—Manager Dusty Baker of the Reds

"The way he hits is just like a samurai. I'll bet he could split a mosquito with a sword."
—Tokyo baseball fan Isao Ogata

"You [Ichiro Suzuki] embody all the best of Major League Baseball. ... You have represented the sport magnificently throughout your Hall of Fame career. On and off the field, you are a man of great integrity."

—MLB Commissioner Bud Selig

"Nobody in baseball can get a hit in as many ways as he can."

—Former teammate Bret Boone

"He's the only Japanese player to go to America and be completely accepted by Americans. He's accomplished what so many Japanese players have only dreamed of doing for decades but never been able to do themselves."

—All-time great Sadaharu Oh

go over the fence," Ichiro would say afterward. "And when it didn't, I was really bummed."

His 2008 season didn't quite measure up to 2007, but he still hit .310 with 213 hits. A year later, Ichiro again started his season with the World Baseball Classic, and again he and Japan took home the title. This time the squad defeated South Korea in the championship game, with Ichiro going 3 for 5 in the leadoff position. It was the warmup to a .352 batting average, which included 225 hits.

Honoring Greatness

Ichiro played in the All-Star Game in St. Louis that summer, his ninth straight appearance. He took advantage of the visit to pay his respects at the grave of George Sisler, the former holder of the record for hits in a major-league season. Ichiro brought his wife and some friends who laid flowers on Sisler's grave. "I wanted to do that for a grand upperclassman of the baseball world. I think it's only natural for someone to want to do that, to express my feelings in that way," he said.

In 2010, Ichiro completed a memorable decade with the Mariners. He hit .315 with 214 hits. He had compiled at least 200 hits in each season with Seattle (leading the league in the category seven times), and his batting average never dropped below .300. Ichiro went 10 for 10 in All-Star appearances, 10 for 10 in Gold Gloves. He turned thirty-seven shortly after the end of the season.

"I don't know if I've earned relaxing time or what, but I think my mind has been at ease after I completed 10 years of play in the majors," he said. Ichiro also told the *Kyodo News*, "Hitting is always an adjustment. The word 'difficult' is not enough to explain what hitting is. Hitting is never easy."

He had made it look easy for those 10 seasons, but finally age started to catch up with him in 2011. Ichiro only hit .272 with 184 hits, including a .210 average in the month of May. His streaks of All-Star appearances and 200-hit seasons came to an end.

With his contract due to expire at the end of the 2012 season, the Mariners had decisions to make. They hadn't made the playoffs since that magical 2001 season, and they had won 67 games in 2011. The Mariners needed to rebuild their team, and a thirty-seven-year-old outfielder couldn't be a part of their long-term plans. But such separations are complicated and never too easy, as all sides discovered in the following season.

Chapter 5

Changes of Scenery

I t was the summer of 2012, and the Seattle Mariners were once again going nowhere.

On July 15 they had a record of 37–53, which put them 17.5 games behind in the American League West. Clearly, there would be no postseason baseball in Seattle again that fall. The Mariners hadn't made the playoffs since 2001, and they had only come within 10 games of a postseason berth twice in that span (2003 and 2006).

What's more, Ichiro Suzuki wasn't helping the Mariners too much. His batting average had dropped into the .260s, and he was earning $17 million per season. At thirty-eight, it appeared that his days as a superstar outfielder had come to an end. Ichiro's contract would expire at the end of the season, and the Mariners knew that he wasn't going to be part of their rebuilding plans.

Seattle decided to see if it could trade Ichiro to another major-league team in order to acquire something for him, as opposed to letting him walk away for nothing at the end of the year. The trading

Opposite: It was odd to see Ichiro in a Yankee uniform after he played more than ten seasons with the Mariners.

deadline was on July 31. Ichiro, like so many other players in that situation, would be willing to go to a new team if it were a contender.

By coincidence, one showed up in Safeco Field about a week before the deadline. The New York Yankees arrived for a three-game series on July 23. They were seven games ahead of the Baltimore Orioles in the American League East, and they had the best record in baseball at 58–38. What's more, they needed an extra outfielder because of a season-ending elbow injury to Brett Gardner. It was a good fit. The Mariners gave up Ichiro and cash for minor-league pitchers D. J. Mitchell and Danny Farquhar.

Ichiro merely had to go to a different locker room when he reported for work on that Monday night. He was immediately put in the lineup in right field, replacing the injured Nick Swisher, and hit eighth. It was the first time in his major league career that he ever hit lower than third in the order. Ichiro came up to the plate in the top of the third inning, and he received a forty-five second standing ovation from the Mariners' crowd. After bowing twice to the crowd, Ichiro ripped a single and stole second base. He finished 1 for 4 as the Yankees defeated Seattle, 4–1.

Going to a Winner

After the game, Ichiro explained his motivation for leaving Seattle. "When I spent time during the All-Star break to think, I realized that this team has many players in their early 20s," Ichiro said through a translator. "I began to think I should not be on this team next year. I also started to feel a desire to be in an atmosphere that I could have a different kind of stimulation than I have right now. … I'm going from a team that has been having the most losses to a team

Ichiro reached the postseason for the second time when he played for the New York Yankees in 2012. His teams never reached the World Series.

Changes of Scenery

that has the most wins, so it's been hard to contain my excitement in that regard."

Mariners executive Chuck Armstrong said, "Ichiro knows that the club is building for the future. He felt that what was best for the team was to be traded to another club and give our younger players an opportunity to develop."

The deal worked out quite well for Ichiro. If he believed that a pennant race would help him play better, he turned out to be correct. The outfielder was a good fit in New York. His batting stroke returned, as he hit .322 in 67 games over the balance of the season. Ichiro also stole 14 bases, which led the team despite the fact he was on the team for only a little more than two months. He played all three outfield positions. Ichiro's combined batting average for the two teams was .283. For a reported $2 million—Seattle picked up the rest of his salary—New York received a good deal.

The Yankees built their lead in the American League East to 8.5 games on July 28 but saw it slip away despite Ichiro's efforts. On September 4, the Orioles and Yankees were tied for first in the division, and the Tampa Bay Rays were close behind. New York was in a tie for the division lead entering the regular season's final week, and it closed with a four-game winning streak to reach the playoffs.

The Yankees drew the Orioles in the first round of the playoffs, and the two teams appropriately battled on equal terms. It took all five games for New York to finish off Baltimore and advance. Ichiro finished with only a .217 batting average in 23 at-bats. He and the Yankees played Detroit next. The Yankees scored 4 runs in the bottom of the ninth in Game One—two coming on a homer by Ichiro—but still lost in 11 innings. That set the tone for the series, as the Tigers swept the Yankees out of the playoffs in four games. Ichiro hit .353 for the series against Detroit.

With the season over and his contract expired, Ichiro went through the task of seeing what might happen to him in free agency. Any team could now sign him, and there was some interest in the marketplace. However, the Yankees had the inside track with Ichiro. He had played well there, and the job in right field was his for the taking. Philadelphia is said to have offered Ichiro more money—$14 million over two years—than the Yankees, but Ichiro accepted a reported two-year, $13 million deal to stay put.

"I believe the Yankees organization appreciates that there is a difference between a thirty-nine-year-old who has played relying only on talent, and a thirty-nine-year-old who has prepared, practiced, and thought thoroughly through many experiences for their craft," Ichiro said. "I am very thankful, and I will do my best to deliver on their expectations."

Most of the 2013 season turned out to be forgettable for Ichiro. The Yankees were a winning team but didn't make the playoffs. The veteran outfielder returned to the level that he had played in 2012 in Seattle, hitting .261 without much power. But there was one moment that stood out.

Milestone Hit

On August 21, Ichiro slapped a single to left field in the bottom of the first inning of a game against the Toronto Blue Jays. The Yankee dugout emptied to congratulate the veteran on the 4,000th hit of his professional career. He had piled up 1,278 hits in Japan, and at

Yankee teammates congratulate Ichiro on his four-thousandth hit as a professional baseball player.

that point had 2,742 in North America. Only two other players, Pete Rose and Ty Cobb, had ever reached 4,000 hits as a pro. Ichiro modestly said that he didn't belong in that sort of company, since he didn't play his entire career in one league. But one of his teammates wasn't buying it.

"That's a lot of hits, man. It's pretty impressive," said Derek Jeter, who would retire with 3,465 hits of his own. "I don't care if it's 4,000 in Little League. It shows how consistent he's been throughout his career. It makes you look at how many hits he's got here [in the Majors] in a short amount of time. That's difficult to do, so Ichiro has been as consistent as anyone."

Ichiro came back for the 2014 season. The Yankees had hopes of using him as more of a fourth outfielder, a spare part in a sense. But Carlos Beltran, the team's usual designated hitter, was hurt and played in only 109 games. That forced manager Joe Girardi to shuffle his lineup, and Ichiro had to play more than most expected. He hit .284, but drove in only 22 runs in 359 at-bats. The Yankees' season ended on a ceremonial note, as Derek Jeter played his final game before retiring. It was fair to ask if Ichiro had played his last game on that same Sunday afternoon in Boston.

While his time in New York was over, Ichiro wasn't quite done with baseball yet. The Miami Marlins pursued him in the offseason and signed the veteran to a one-year contract worth $2 million. The Marlins had a top young outfield, and they hoped Ichiro could pass along his experience. In spring training in 2015, Ichiro hinted that his time in New York had not ended well, and he was hoping for a fresh start in South Florida.

"I'm 41. I obviously don't know what my role is right now," he said. "I'll go through camp and find that out. Hopefully, it won't look like I'm using a bat as a cane."

Ichiro again probably saw more playing time than he should have received in 2015, but injuries and other issues made it a necessity. He hit only .229, easily the worst figure of his career. Ichiro did receive plenty of attention for something he did at the end of the season, pitching an inning against the Phillies. He allowed one run and one hit. "To be on the mound at a Major League Baseball game, you can say one of my dreams came true today," he said after the game. "But I'll never ask to do that again."

The Marlins signed him once again to be a spare outfielder for 2016 and cut down his playing time. Ichiro's at-bats dropped from 398 to 327, and the extra rest apparently did him some good. He hit .291, his best batting average since 2010 with the Mariners. Ichiro also had a couple of moments along the way that made baseball history.

Historical Debate

The first started something of an argument. Ichiro had two hits on June 15 in San Diego to raise his career hit total in both Japan and the United States to 4,257. That was the largest number in baseball history, passing Pete Rose. "For me, it's not about the record," Ichiro said. "It's about my teammates and the fans, the way they reacted. That meant a lot to me."

He received a big ovation from the twenty thousand fans in San Diego. The one person who wasn't applauding the achievement was Rose, who made it clear earlier in the month in an interview with *USA Today* that he wasn't impressed. "It sounds like in Japan, they're trying to make me the 'Hit Queen,'" Rose said. "I'm not trying to take anything away from Ichiro, he's had a Hall of Fame career, but the next thing you know, they'll be counting his high school hits."

Ichiro takes a well-deserved bow after recording the three-thousandth hit of his major league baseball career.

Ichiro Suzuki: A League of His Own

Marlins president David Samson didn't agree. "If you could have twenty-five Ichiros, you would have twenty-five World Series rings," Samson said. "He is a true, humble professional who works as hard when he's 0 for 5 as when he's 5 for 5. That skill cannot be taught."

The hits left Ichiro only 29 away from reaching 3,000 in the major leagues, and the countdown was officially on. The number was almost difficult to imagine, mostly because Ichiro had arrived in Seattle at the age of twenty-seven. "To think in that first year that this young man would be playing at forty-two and going for 3,000 hits, I didn't think it was possible then," said Lou Piniella, the manager of the 2001 Mariners. "Just 2,000 hits would have been an outstanding achievement."

Former Yankees teammate Robinson Cano credited Ichiro's work ethic for making such a remarkable achievement possible. "You would have to kick him out of baseball. Because he works out every day," he said to ESPN. "Even when he's in the batting cage, he had his own weights he would lift before he hit. He was in shape. That's the guy you're never going to see retire. He loves baseball so much. He said, 'I'm going to play until I'm fifty years old.' If you're close to a milestone, why retire?"

The wait ended on August 7, and the milestone hit turned out to be memorable. Ichiro became the thirtieth major league player to reach 3,000 hits, and only the second one to do it with a triple. It took him sixteen seasons, faster than anyone other than Rose. The veteran also was the first Asian-born player to reach the number, and the fourth born outside of the United States (Rod Carew, Roberto Clemente, and Rafael Palmeiro were the others).

After the game, Ichiro said:

Ichiro Suzuki Scorecard

Career Highlights: Won seven straight batting championships in Japan (1994–2000); became the thirtieth player in Major League Baseball history to have 3,000 hits in his career (2016); won two American League batting championships (2001 and 2004); led the American League in hits seven times (2001, 2004, 2006–2010); set a Seattle Mariners team record with 2,533 career hits; member of the winning team in the World Baseball Classic in 2005 and 2009; set the MLB record for hits in a season with 262 (2004); set the record for most hits as a professional (Japanese league or MLB) in baseball history; reached 200 hits for ten consecutive seasons (2001–2010), breaking Ty Cobb's American League record for career seasons of 200 hits, and tying Pete Rose's major league record; had seven streaks of twenty or more games with at least one hit, an American League record.

Firsts: First Japanese-born non-pitcher to be posted and signed by a major league team (2000); first Major League Baseball player to enter the Japanese Baseball Hall of Fame (2007).

Honors: Won three consecutive Most Valuable Player awards in the Pacific League in Japan (1994–1996); named American League Rookie of the Year and Most Valuable Player in the same year (2001); won ten straight Gold Glove Awards for fielding excellence (2001–2010), only Roberto Clemente and Willie Mays have won more in a row (twelve each) in the outfield; appeared in ten straight All-Star Games (2001–2010); won the 2007 MVP award in the All-Star Game, a game in which he hit the first inside-the-park homer in the event's history.

It hasn't been too long since Japanese players started to come over here to play in the major leagues. There are still just very few. I've come here and I've been able to get some hits. ... There's more we need to do as Japanese players. But hopefully this three thousandth hit will bring that bridge closer, and that maybe we'll be able to have the Japanese players and also the Americans, the fans, understand that Japanese baseball is good baseball.

At the end of the 2016 season, it was difficult to put Ichiro's career into some sort of historical perspective. There had been fifty-four Japanese players who crossed the Pacific to play in the majors. Some were still playing in 2016. Ichiro was the biggest name on the active list because of his superb career, but only Nori Aoki and Munenori Kawasaki joined him on a list of **position players** from Japan. The active pitchers at the time were better known; Yu Darvish, Hisaski Iwakuma, Masahiro Tanaka, Koji Uehara, Junichi Tazawa, and Kenta Maeda enjoyed some success in North America.

The non-pitchers on the all-time list have had their struggles in Major League Baseball. The biggest success story is Hideki Matsui, who spent ten years playing in Japan before jumping to the New York Yankees. He played seven seasons there (2003 to 2009). Matsui is remembered for hitting a grand slam in his first game as a Yankee. He won the Most Valuable Player Award for the 2009 World Series. The outfielder spent three more years in North America with other teams.

"He came here and was supposed to be this Godzilla that hits home runs, but he was a situational hitter," Yankees teammate Derek

Ichiro Suzuki: A League of His Own

Jeter said. "Matsui moved runners when he had to move them, he got big hits, he drove guys in, he wanted to play every day. The biggest thing—he never made excuses. Never heard him talk about any injuries, which I appreciate—he would play or he didn't play. I enjoyed getting to know him throughout the years. He's always been one of my favorite teammates and always will be."

Others weren't so lucky. Kosuke Fukudome came to the Chicago Cubs in 2008 with considerable fanfare. He stayed in North America for five seasons but struggled and returned to Japan. Kaz Matsui was a superb infielder for the Seibu Lions in Japan for nine seasons, joining the New York Mets in 2004. But he had little success and returned home in 2011.

Was Ichiro a true pioneer, or a one-of-a-kind player whose journey from Japan to North America will never be duplicated? It's too early to tell. It remains to be seen how others will do as they try to make an impact on Major League Baseball in North America.

No matter what his legacy, though, Ichiro always will be considered an extraordinary player. He certainly was a model citizen during his time in the big leagues. Ichiro always kept himself in top shape, doing extra workouts beyond what was asked of him. That allowed him to join an exclusive group of major leaguers who have played some center field past the age of forty. Ichiro got along well with teammates and even went to the trouble of learning to speak English and Spanish.

He also proved generous to both his old home and his new one. In 2011, when Japan was hit with the tsunami that devastated portions of that country, Ichiro donated $1.24 million to the relief effort. The veteran has given a great deal of memorabilia to the

Baseball Hall of Fame in Cooperstown over the years, although he did keep the bat that was used for his three thousandth hit.

Ichiro himself will be inducted one day at the shrine in Cooperstown, but no one could say for sure when that might take place. He must wait for five years after retiring from the game. The Marlins delayed that process by at least a year when they signed him for 2017 shortly after the end of the 2016 season.

"He wants to play until he's fifty," the Marlins' David Samson said. "He's told me. He's serious. I think he probably will play until he's fifty, and that's fine by us."

Timeline

October 22, 1973 Born in Kasugai, Japan

1991 Participates in The Koshien, Japan's national high school baseball championship.

November 1991 The Orix BlueWave select Ichiro in the fourth and final round of the Professional Baseball Draft.

1992 Plays his first professional game with the BlueWave.

1994 Becomes a regular for Orix. Ichiro sets a league record for hits in a season and wins the batting title.

1995 Participates in Japan's version of the World Series.

1996 Wins his third consecutive Most Valuable Player Award in Japan, and his team wins the Japan Series championship.

December 3, 1999 Marries sportscaster Yumiko Fukushima.

November 19, 2000 After winning his seventh straight batting title, Ichiro signs with the Seattle Mariners.

April 2, 2001 Makes his major league debut.

October 2001 Becomes the second player to win the Most Valuable Player and Rookie of the Year awards in the same season.

October 1, 2004 Breaks George Sisler's major league record for hits in a season with his 258th hit. He finishes with 262 and wins his second batting championship.

March 20, 2006 Gets two hits and scores three runs as Japan beats Cuba, 10–6, to win the inaugural World Baseball Classic.

July 10, 2007 Wins the Most Valuable Player Award in the All-Star Game.

March 23, 2009 Japan wins its second World Baseball Classic title with a 5–3 victory over Korea. Ichiro shares tournament lead with two others with twelve hits.

September 23, 2010 Reaches 200 hits in a season for the tenth straight season, tying a major-league record. He also wins his tenth straight Gold Glove for fielding excellence.

July 23, 2012 Mariners trade Ichiro to the New York Yankees.

January 27, 2015 Miami Marlins announce the signing of Ichiro to a free-agent contract.

June 15, 2016 Ichiro gets two hits to tie then break Pete Rose's record of 4,256 career hits in professional baseball. Ichiro's totals include 1,278 hits with Orix.

August 7, 2016 Ichiro triples for his 3,000th major-league hit, the thirtieth player to reach that number. He finishes the season with 3,030 hits in MLB and 4,308 for his career.

Glossary

batting cage An area used for practicing hitting that is enclosed by wire or netting.

bullpen The area that is used by baseball's relief pitchers to warm up before entering games. It also can refer to a team's relief pitchers as a group.

closer A relief pitcher who is used to record the final outs of the game when his team is ahead, thus ensuring a victory.

Cy Young Award An award that given to the best pitcher in the American and National League each year. Baseball reporters who write for newspapers vote for the winners.

earned-run average A statistic that measures the average number of earned runs allowed by a pitcher per nine innings (the equivalent of a complete game). For example, if the pitcher allows two runs in eighteen innings, his earned-run average would be 1.00.

free agency A time when a player who does not have a contract and can sign with any team.

hazing Forcing individuals to take part in strenuous, humiliating, or dangerous tasks.

kimono A long, loose robe, once used by the Japanese in formal occasions.

loophole An ambiguity in a set of rules or a contract that allows someone to exercise a right.

militarism The belief of a government that a country should maintain a strong military capability and to use it aggressively to promote national interests.

Negro Leagues A group of baseball teams consisting of players who were either African American or Latino at a time when people of color were not allowed to play in the Major Leagues. The Negro Leagues thrived in the 1930s and 1940s until Major League Baseball allowed blacks and Latinos to play on its teams, starting in 1947.

Nomo clause Refers to a change in the contracts of Japanese baseball players, caused by the move by Hideo Nomo to the Los Angeles Dodgers in 1995. Japanese players no longer were considered free to sign with any team throughout the world by filing retirement papers in their home country.

offseasons The time between the end of the competition season, and the beginning of training camp before the following season.

on-base percentage A measure of how often a baseball player reaches base safely. It is approximately calculated by adding hits, walks, and hit-by-pitch plays, and dividing the total by all plate appearances. A .400 on-base percentage is excellent.

Pearl Harbor The harbor near Honolulu on the island of Oahu in Hawaii. The site of a large naval base, it was attacked by Japanese forces on December 7, 1941. The action started America's involvement in World War II.

position players The non-pitching players on a baseball team's roster. They also are called everyday players.

rookie A first-year player in a sport.

slugging percentage A measure of a baseball batter's power. It is calculated by dividing total bases (one for a single, two for a double, etc.) by at-bats. Thirty-five players had a slugging percentage of .500 or better (one half of a base per at-bat) in the 2016 baseball season.

tendinitis The inflammation of a tendon, usually caused by overuse.

yen Japan's unit of currency, the equivalent to America's dollar. In 2016, 1,000 yen was worth $8.76.

Bibliography

Books

Beach, Jerry. *Godzilla Takes the Bronx.* Lanham, MD: Taylor Trade Publishing, 2004.

Leigh, David S. *Ichiro Suzuki.* Minneapolis, MN: Twenty-First Century Books, 2012

Whiting, Robert. *The Meaning of Ichiro.* New York: Warner Books, 2004.

Online Articles

Anderson, David. "When Bay-bee Ruth toured Japan." *New York Times,* March 26, 2000. http://www.nytimes.com/2000/03/26/sports/sports-of-the-times-when-bay-bee-ruth-toured-japan.html?_r=0.

Andriesen, David. "Ichiro breaks 84-year-old record for hits in a season." *Seattle Post-Intelligencer,* October 1, 2004. http://www.seattlepi.com/sports/article/Ichiro-breaks-84-year-old-record-for-hits-in-a-1155680.php.

AZ Quotes. "Ichiro Suzuki Quotes." Accessed November 22, 2016. http://www.azquotes.com/author/14337-Ichiro_Suzuki.

"Babe's 1934 Barnstorming Trip to Japan." Babe Ruth Central. Accessed October 24, 2016. http://www.baberuthcentral.com/babesimpact/babe-ruths-legacy/babes-1934-barnstorming-trip-to-japan.

Baseball Almanac. "Ichiro Suzuki Quotes." Accessed October 31, 2016. http://www.baseball-almanac.com/quotes/ichiro_suzuki_quotes.shtml.

Caple, Jim. "Ichiro, Matsui hit center stage." ESPN, April 30, 2003. http://www.espn.com/mlb/columns/story?id=1546467.

————— "Ichiro reaches 3,000 hits by following meticulous standards." ESPN, August 7, 2016. http://www.espn.com/mlb/story/_/id/17127981/ichiro-reaches-3000-hits-following-meticulous-standards.

Casella, Paul. "Ichiro's 4K milestone one of 2013's top moments." MLB.com, December 22, 2013. http://m.mlb.com/news/article/66131254.

David, Craig, and Tim Healey. "Marlins' Ichiro Suzuki becomes 30th player with 3,000 hits." *Sun-Sentinel*: August 7, 2016. http://www.sun-sentinel.com/sports/miami-marlins/sfl-ichiro-suzuki-3000-hits-miami-marlins-20160729-story.html.

Eder, Steve. "Reds, media follow Ichiro." *Cincinnati Enquirer*, June 20, 2002. http://reds.enquirer.com/2002/06/20/red_fans_media_follow.html.

"The First of Many." National Baseball Hall of Fame. Accessed October 25, 2016. http://baseballhall.org/discover/the-first-of-many

Gulizia, Anthony. "Masha Murakami, MLB Pioneer." *Guardian*, July 1, 2015. https://www.theguardian.com/sport/2015/jul/01/mashi-murakami-japan-mlb-baseball.

"Ichiro looks back on 2010 season." *Japan Times*. December 21, 2010. http://www.japantimes.co.jp/sports/2010/12/21/baseball/mlb/ichiro-looks-back-on-2010-season.

"Ichiro Suzuki—What They Say." Jockbio.com. Accessed November 29, 2016. http://www.jockbio.com/Bios/Suzuki_Ichiro/Ichiro_they-say.html.

"Ichiro visits Sisler's grave." ESPN. July 15, 2009. http://www.espn.com/mlb/news/story?id=4329684.

Kernan, Kevin. "Why Ichiro is glad to be a Marlin, and away from Joe Girardi." *New York Post*. February 25, 2015. http://nypost.com/2015/02/25/why-ichiro-is-glad-to-be-a-marlin-and-away-from-joe-girardi.

"Koshien Heroes." PBS. Accessed October 31, 2016. http://www.pbs.org/pov/kokoyakyu/koshien-heroes/2.

Mandich, Steve. "Super Ichiro Crazy." Accessed November 14, 2016. http://www.stevemandich.com/otherstuff/ichiro.htm.

McKenna, Brian. "Lefty O'Doul." Society for American Baseball Research. Accessed October 24, 2016. http://sabr.org/bioproj/person/b820a06c.

Morosi, John Paul. "Ichiro climbs high to deny." *Seattle Post-Intelligencer*. May 2, 2005. http://www.seattlepi.com/sports/baseball/article/Ichiro-climbs-high-to-deny-1172392.php.

O'Kennedy, Patrick. "The Legend of Lefty O'Doul." SB Nation. March 17, 2014. http://www.blessyouboys.com/2014/3/17/5503558/the-legend-of-lefty-odoul.

Pearlman, Jeff. "Big Hit." *Sports Illustrated*. May 28, 2001. http://www.si.com/vault/2001/05/28/304347/big-hit-fans-have-quickly-gotten-on-a-first-name-basis-with-ichiro-the-brilliant-batsman-and-dazzling-all-around-talent-from-japan-who-has-led-the-mariners-to-the-top-of-the-american-league.

Price, S. L. "The Ichiro Paradox." *Sports Illustrated*. July 8, 2002. http://www.si.com/vault/2002/07/08/326024/the-ichiro-paradox-no-power-no-personality-yet-with-no-peer-the-mariners-ichiro-suzuki-may-be-the-greatest-player-to-come-out-of-japan-and-the-worst-thing-to-happen-to-japanese-baseball.

Reilly, Rick. "Itching for Ichiro." *Sports Illustrated*. September 17, 2001. http://www.si.com/vault/2001/09/17/310745/itching-for-ichiro.

Schoenfield, David. "2001 Mariners: Best team that never won." ESPN. September 12, 2011. http://www.espn.com/blog/sweetspot/post/_/id/16050/2001-mariners-best-team-that-never-won.

"Some Trivia about Ichiro's 262-Hit Season in 2004." Misc. Baseball. Accessed February 15, 2010. https://miscbaseball.wordpress.com/2010/02/15/some-trivia-about-ichiros-262-hit-season-in-2004.

Spencer, Clark. "Ichiro passes Pete Rose with 4,257 combined hits as Marlins fall to Padres." *Miami Herald,* June 15, 2016. http://www.miamiherald.com/sports/mlb/miami-marlins/article83967877.html.

―――. "Kisses aside, Ichiro Suzuki still enjoys Opening Day." *Miami Herald,* April 6, 2016. http://www.miamiherald.com/sports/mlb/miami-marlins/article70286362.html.

Stone, Larry. "How Ichiro proved to Lou Piniella he belonged that spring of 2001." *Seattle Times.* July 9, 2011. http://www.seattletimes.com/sports/mariners/how-ichiro-proved-to-lou-piniella-he-belonged-that-spring-of-2001.

Wilson, Bernie. "Analysis: Classic cautiously called a hit." *Seattle Post-Intelligencer.* March 21, 2006. http://www.seattlepi.com/sports/baseball/article/Analysis-Classic-cautiously-ruled-a-hit-1199089.php.

"Yankees acquire Ichiro Suzuki." ESPN. July 24, 2012. http://www.espn.com/new-york/mlb/story/_/id/8193142/new-york-yankees-acquire-ichiro-suzuki-seattle-mariners.

Further Information

Books

Beach, Jerry. *Godzilla Takes the Bronx.* Lanham, MD: Taylor Trade Publishing, 2004.

Christopher, Matt, and Glenn Stout. *At the Plate with Ichiro.* Boston: Little, Brown, 2003.

Fitts, Robert K. *Banzai Babe Ruth.* Lincoln, NE: University of Nebraska Press, 2012.

Suzuki, Ichiro. *Ichiro on Ichiro.* Seattle, WA: Sasquatch, 2004.

Whiting, Robert. *The Chrysanthemum and the Bat: The Game Japanese Play.* New York: Dodd, Mead, 1977.

———. *The Meaning of Ichiro.* New York: Warner Books, 2004.

Websites

Baseball Reference: Ichiro Suzuki

http://www.baseball-reference.com/players/s/suzukic01.shtml

Read all of Ichiro's MLB statistics

Biography: Ichiro Suzuki

http://www.biography.com/people/ichiro-suzuki-37219#synopsis

Biography provides a quick read on the life of Ichiro Suzuki.

Super Ichiro Crazy

http://www.stevemandich.com/otherstuff/ichiro.htm

This fan page provides "all things Ichiro."

Videos

Ichiro breaks single-season hits record

https://www.youtube.com/watch?v=HL-XjMCPfio.
George Sisler's record had lasted almost a century, until
this moment.

Ichiro's iconic throw to third base

https://www.youtube.com/watch?v=WYAxk01E404
Here's a look at the 2001 throw that showed all of baseball that
Ichiro was one of the best fielders in the game.

Ichiro Suzuki pitching against the Phillies

https://www.youtube.com/watch?v=H80xg3aCx0A
Check out his form during a brief appearance on the mound at the
end of the 2015 season.

3-chiro: 3B for 30th to reach 3,000 hits!

http://m.marlins.mlb.com/news/article/194177132/ichiro-suzuki-
triples-for-3000th-career-hit/
Ichiro's milestone triple was one of the top moments of his career.

Index

Page numbers in **boldface** are illustrations. Entries in **boldface** are glossary terms.

About the Author

Budd Bailey has been a sports reporter and editor for the *Buffalo News* since 1993. Before that, he worked for the Buffalo Sabres hockey team and WEBR Radio, where he served as one of the announcers for the Buffalo Bisons' baseball broadcasts for four seasons. Budd and his wife, Jody, live in Buffalo, New York. This is his eighth book, including five for Cavendish Square.